Contents

Avocado Pistachio Ice Cream

Prep Time: 10 minutes

Cooking Time: 0 minutes

Freezing Time: 4 hours

Servings: 8

Ingredients:
- 1/2 cup coconut oil
- 1/2 cup avocado oil
- 2 tablespoons apple cider vinegar
- 4 egg yolks
- 2 cups full fat coconut milk
- 2 tablespoons grass-fed gelatin
- 1 tablespoon matcha green tea powder
- 1 tablespoon pure vanilla extract
- 1/2 teaspoon ground cinnamon
- 1 pinch Himalayan salt
- 2 large ripe hass avocado
- 1/2 cup raw shelled pistachios, chopped

Directions:
1. Beat egg yolks with apple cider vinegar, avocado oil, and coconut oil in a mixing bowl until it makes a white mayonnaise mixture.
2. Blend coconut milk, vanilla, matcha powder, gelatin, salt, and cinnamon in a blender jug.
3. Stir in prepared mayonnaise, and avocado mash then blend until smooth.
4. Transfer this mixture to the ice-cream mixer
5. Churn and freeze the ice-cream according to the machine's instructions.
6. Add pistachios to the ice-cream and mix them evenly.
7. Freeze the pistachio ice-cream again for 1 hour.
8. Serve and enjoy.

Nutritional Values: Calories 286 Total Fat 28.2g Saturated Fat 14.4g Cholesterol 105mg Sodium 35mg Total Carbohydrate 8.2g Dietary Fiber 4.5g Total Sugars 0.6g Protein 4.4g

Butter Pecan Ice Cream

Prep Time: 10 minutes

Cooking Time: 10 minutes

Freezing Time: 4 hours

Servings: 8

Ingredients:

- 1/4 cup butter
- 2 cups heavy cream
- 1/4 cup Erythritol
- 1/4 cup liquid Allulose
- 1/4 teaspoon salt
- 2 egg yolks
- 2 teaspoon choc zero maple extract
- 1 tablespoon MCT oil
- 2 tablespoons pecans toasted, chopped

Directions:
1. Place a suitable pan on medium-low heat and melt butter in it until it turns brown.
2. Mix this butter with chopped pecans, heavy cream, erythritol, and Allulose in a suitable bowl.
3. Stir in cream, salt, maple extract, and MCT oil, then beat well until fluffy.
4. Beat egg yolks in a suitable bowl until creamy and add to the cream mixture.
5. Transfer this mixture to the ice-cream mixer.
6. Churn and freeze the ice-cream according to the machine's instructions.
7. Fold in pecans and mix gently until evenly incorporated.
8. Freeze the butter-pecan ice-cream for 1 hour.
9. Serve and enjoy.

Nutritional Values: Calories 203   Total Fat 21.7g Saturated Fat 11g Cholesterol 56mg Sodium 126mg Total Carbohydrate 9.2g Dietary Fiber 0.6g Total Sugars 7.7g Protein 1.4g

Mixed Berry Ice Cream

Prep Time: 10 minutes

Cooking Time: 0 minutes

Freezing Time: 2 hours

Servings: 2

Ingredients:
- ½ cup frozen blueberries
- ½ cup of frozen strawberries
- 1/2 cup heavy cream
- 1/8 teaspoon stevia powder

Directions:
1. Blend berries, cream and stevia in a blender until smooth.
2. Transfer this mixture to the ice-cream mixer.
3. Freeze this berry cream mixture for 2 hours in the freezer.
4. Serve and enjoy.

Nutritional Values: Calories 137   Total Fat 11.2g Saturated Fat 6.9g Cholesterol 41mg Sodium 12mg Total Carbohydrate 9.3g Dietary Fiber 1.6g Total Sugars 5.9g Protein 0.9g

Death by Chocolate Ice Cream

Prep Time: 10 minutes

Cooking Time: 10 minutes

Freezing Time: 4 hours

Servings: 8

Ingredients:
- 1 1/2 cups heavy cream
- 3/4 cups unsweetened almond milk
- 1/3 cup dark cocoa powder
- 1/3 cup Erythritol Sweetener
- 1/3 cup xylitol
- 3 large egg yolks
- 2 oz. unsweetened chocolate chopped
- 1/2 teaspoon vanilla extract
- 1/8 teaspoon salt

Directions:
1. Mix cream with almond milk, sweeteners, and cocoa powder in a saucepan.
2. Heat cocoa cream mixture until it reaches 160 degrees F.
3. Beat egg yolks in a medium bowl and pour in 1 cup cream mixture.
4. Whisk well, then return this mixture to the saucepan.
5. Cook this mixture with occasional stirring, until it thickens.
6. Remove the ice-cream mixture from the heat and add the chopped chocolate.
7. Mix well and leave this mixture to cool at room temperature.
8. Transfer this mixture to the ice-cream mixer.
9. Churn and freeze the ice-cream according to the machine's instructions.
10. Serve and enjoy.

Nutritional Values: Calories 138 Total Fat 14.1g Saturated Fat 8.1g Cholesterol 110mg Sodium 68mg Total Carbohydrate 3.3g Dietary Fiber 1.4g Total Sugars 0.2g Protein 2.5 g

Chocolate Peanut Butter Ice Cream

Prep Time: 10 minutes

Cooking Time: 0 minutes

Freezing Time: 4 hours

Servings: 6

Ingredients:
- 1 (13.5-oz can) coconut milk
- 1/2 cup peanut butter

- 1/3 cup coconut oil
- 1/4 cup cocoa powder
- 1/2 cup powdered Allulose
- 1 pinch sea salt

Directions:
1. Blend coconut milk, peanut butter, coconut oil, cocoa powder, allulose, and salt in a blender until smooth.
2. Transfer this mixture to the ice-cream mixer.
3. Churn and freeze the ice-cream according to the machine's instructions.
4. Serve and enjoy.

Nutritional Values: Calories 252 Total Fat 24.1g Saturated Fat 13.9g Cholesterol 0mg Sodium 146mg Total Carbohydrate 7.8g Dietary Fiber 2.4g Total Sugars 2.1g Protein 7.2g

Pumpkin Ice Cream

Prep Time: 10 minutes

Cooking Time: 10 minutes

Freezing Time: 6 hours

Servings: 8

Ingredients:
- 2 cups heavy whipping cream
- 1/3 cup brown erythritol
- 1/3 cup xylitol
- 1 teaspoon instant espresso powder
- 4 large egg yolks
- 1 teaspoon ground cinnamon
- 1/2 teaspoon ground ginger
- 1/8 teaspoon ground cloves
- 1 cup pumpkin puree
- 1 teaspoon vanilla extract

Directions:
1. Mix cream with erythritol, xylitol, espresso powder, cinnamon, ginger ground, cloves ground, and vanilla extract in a saucepan.
2. Heat spiced cream mixture until it reaches 160 degrees F.
3. Beat egg yolks in a medium bowl and pour in 1 cup cream mixture.
4. Whisk well, then return this mixture to the saucepan.
5. Cook this mixture with occasional stirring, until it thickens.
6. Remove the ice-cream mixture from the heat and add pumpkin puree.
7. Mix well and leave this mixture to cool at room temperature.
8. Transfer this mixture to the ice-cream mixer
9. Churn and freeze the ice-cream according to the machine's instructions.

10. Serve and enjoy.

Nutritional Values: Calories 144   Total Fat 13.5g Saturated Fat 7.8g Cholesterol 146mg Sodium 17mg Total Carbohydrate 4g Dietary Fiber 1.1g Total Sugars 1.2g Protein 2.3g

Vanilla Pops

Prep Time: 10 minutes

Cooking Time: 10 minutes

Freezing Time: 4 hours

Servings: 8

Ingredients:
- 1 cup whipping cream
- 1/2 cup unsweetened almond milk
- 3 large egg yolks
- 6 tablespoon erythritol
- Pinch salt
- 2 tablespoons butter, cut into two pieces
- 1 1/2 teaspoon vanilla extract
- 1/4 teaspoon xanthan gum

Directions:
1. Mix almond milk and cream in a saucepan and cook the mixture to a simmer.
2. Beat egg yolks with erythritol and salt in a mixing bowl.
3. Stir in half of the hot milk mixture and mix well with the egg yolks.
4. Pour this mixture back into the pan and continue mixing and until the milk thickens.
5. Remove this milk-cream mixture from the heat.
6. Stir in vanilla extract, butter, xanthan gum, and mix well.
7. Divide the mixture into the popsicle molds.
8. Insert the popsicle sticks and freeze these popsicles for 4 hours.
9. Remove the popsicles from their molds.
10. Serve immediately.

Nutritional Values: Calories 94   Total Fat 9.4g Saturated Fat 5.4g Cholesterol 103mg Sodium 59mg Total Carbohydrate 9.9g Dietary Fiber 0.1g Total Sugars 0.2g Protein 1

Strawberry Rhubarb Pops

Prep Time: 10 minutes

Cooking Time: 5 minutes

Freezing Time: 3 hours

Servings: 6

Ingredients:
- 1 1/2 cups rhubarb, chopped
- 3/4 cup strawberries, chopped
- 2 tablespoons water
- 6 tablespoon erythritol
- 1/2 cup heavy whipping cream
- 1/2 teaspoon vanilla extract

Directions:
1. Mix strawberries, water, 3 tablespoons erythritol, and rhubarb in a saucepan.
2. Cook this berry mixture to a boil then reduce its heat. Cook for 5 minutes.
3. Mash all the berries with a fork and- leave the mixture to cool.
4. Beat cream with remaining erythritol and vanilla extract in a mixing bowl.
5. Gently stir in the strawberry mixture and mix gently to make swirls.
6. Divide the mixture into the popsicle molds.
7. Insert the popsicle sticks and freeze these popsicles for 3 hours.
8. Remove the popsicles from their molds.
9. Serve immediately.

Nutritional Values: Calories 51   Total Fat 3.8g Saturated Fat 2.3g Cholesterol 14mg Sodium 5mg

Total Carbohydrate 5.8g Dietary Fiber 1.1g Total Sugars 1.7g Protein 0.7g

Chocolate Cheesecake Popsicles

Prep Time: 10 minutes

Cooking Time: 0 minutes

Freezing Time: 5 hours

Servings: 5

Ingredients:
- 4 oz. cream cheese
- 1/2 cup coconut milk
- 1/4 cup erythritol
- 1-oz. unsweetened chocolate, melted
- 1 teaspoon vanilla extract

Directions:
1. Blend cream cheese with erythritol, coconut milk, melted chocolate, and vanilla extract in a blender.
2. Divide the mixture into the popsicle molds.
3. Insert the popsicle sticks and freeze these popsicles for 5 hours.
4. Remove the popsicles from their molds.
5. Serve immediately.

Nutritional Values: Calories 165   Total Fat 16.6g Saturated Fat 11.9g Cholesterol 25mg Sodium

72mg Total Carbohydrate 3.9g Dietary Fiber 1.5g Total Sugars 1g Protein 3g

Coffee Popsicles

Prep Time: 10 minutes

Cooking Time: 0 minutes

Freezing Time: 3 hours

Servings: 6

Ingredients:
- ½ cup heavy whipping cream, chilled
- 6 tablespoon Erythritol
- ½ teaspoon vanilla extract
- 1 cup brewed coffee, chilled

Directions:
1. Blend cream, erythritol, vanilla extract, and brewed coffee in a blender.
2. Divide the coffee mixture into the popsicle molds.
3. Insert the popsicle sticks and freeze these popsicles for 3 hours.
4. Remove the popsicles from their molds.
5. Serve immediately.

Nutritional Values: Calories 36 Total Fat 3.7g Saturated Fat 2.3g Cholesterol 14mg Sodium 5mg

Total Carbohydrate 10.3g Dietary Fiber 0g Total Sugars 0.1g Protein 0.3g

Blueberry Yogurt Pops

Prep Time: 10 minutes

Cooking Time: 0 minutes

Freezing Time: 3 hours

Servings: 4

Ingredients:
- 3 oz frozen blueberries
- 3/4 cup organic full-fat Greek yogurt
- 1/2 cup organic coconut milk
- 30 drops vanilla stevia

Directions:
1. Blend blueberries, yogurt, coconut milk, and stevia in a blender.
2. Divide this blueberry mixture in the popsicle molds.
3. Insert the popsicle sticks and freeze these popsicles for 3 hours.
4. Remove the popsicles from their molds.
5. Serve immediately.

Nutritional Values: Calories 113 Total Fat 8.1g Saturated Fat 7g Cholesterol 4mg Sodium 18mg

Total Carbohydrate 6.4g Dietary Fiber 1.2g Total Sugars 4.8g Protein 5.2g

Mint Ice Cream

Prep Time: 10 minutes

Cooking Time: 10 minutes

Freezing Time: 4 hours

Servings: 6

Ingredients:
- 2 cups heavy whipping cream
- 1/4 cup unsweetened almond milk
- 4 egg yolks
- 5 drops green food coloring
- 3 tablespoons Peppermint extract
- 1/4 teaspoon mint extract
- 1 teaspoon stevia powder

Directions:
1. Mix heavy cream with milk in a saucepan and heat over medium heat.
2. Beat egg yolks with stevia in a suitable bowl until pale and creamy.
3. Add half of the milk-cream mixture to the eggs and mix well.
4. Return the mixture to the pan and cook until it thickens.
5. Transfer this mixture to the ice-cream mixer.
6. Allow the ice-cream mixture to cool then add remaining ingredients.
7. Churn and freeze the ice-cream according to the machine's instructions.
8. Serve and enjoy.

Nutritional Values: Calories 194   Total Fat 18g Saturated Fat 10.3g Cholesterol 195mg Sodium 29mg Total Carbohydrate 2.4g Dietary Fiber 0g Total Sugars 0.9g Protein 2.7g

Toasted Almond Ice Cream

Prep Time: 10 minutes

Cooking Time: 10 minutes

Freezing Time: 6 hours

Servings: 8

Ingredients:
- 3/4 cup erythritol
- 1 3/4 cups almond milk
- 2 cups heavy cream

- Pinch of salt
- 4 egg yolks
- 1 teaspoon vanilla
- 1 teaspoon almond extract
- 1/3 cup crushed roasted almonds

Directions:
1. Add cream and almond milk to a saucepan and heat over medium heat.
2. Beat egg yolks with erythritol and salt in a suitable bowl until pale and creamy.
3. Add half of the cream mixture to the eggs and mix well.
4. Return the mixture to the pan and cook until it thickens.
5. Transfer this mixture to the ice-cream mixer.
6. Allow the ice-cream mixture to cool then add vanilla and almond extracts.
7. Churn and freeze the ice-cream according to the machine's instructions.
8. Stir in roasted almonds and mix well.
9. Freeze the almond ice-cream for 1 hour.
10. Serve and enjoy.

Nutritional Values: Calories 287 Total Fat 28.9g Saturated Fat 19.1g Cholesterol 146mg Sodium 43mg Total Carbohydrate 5.2g Dietary Fiber 1.8g Total Sugars 2.2g Protein 4.4g

Cashew Ice Cream

Prep Time: 10 minutes

Cooking Time: 10 minutes

Freezing Time: 6 hours

Servings: 6

Ingredients:
- 2 cups cashew milk
- 1 cup coconut cream
- 1 cup erythritol
- 1/4 cup water
- 2/3 cup 1 tablespoon cacao butter
- 1/4 cup coconut oil
- 1/2 cup cashew butter
- 1 teaspoon salt

Directions:
1. Add cream and cashew milk to a saucepan and heat over medium heat.
2. Stir in water, cocoa butter, coconut oil, cashew butter, and salt.
3. Mix well and cook this mixture until it thickens.
4. Transfer this mixture to the ice-cream mixer.
5. Allow the ice-cream mixture to cool then add remaining ingredients.
6. Churn and freeze the ice-cream according to the machine's instructions.

7. Serve and enjoy.

Nutritional Values: Calories 244 Total Fat 22.9g Saturated Fat 11.9g Cholesterol 0mg Sodium 451mg Total Carbohydrate 8.4g Dietary Fiber 1.3g Total Sugars 1.3g Protein 5g

Mojito Popsicles

Prep Time: 10 minutes

Cooking Time: 0 minutes

Freezing Time: 3 hours

Servings: 8

Ingredients:
- 2 cups of water
- ½ cup lime juice
- ¼ teaspoon stevia
- 20 mint leaves, cut into ribbons

Directions:
1. Mix water, lime juice, stevia, and mint leaves ribbons in a mason jar.
2. Divide the mixture into the popsicle molds.
3. Insert the popsicle sticks and freeze these popsicles for 3 hours.
4. Remove the popsicles from their molds.
5. Serve immediately.

Nutritional Values: Calories 1 Total Fat 0g Saturated Fat 0g Cholesterol 0mg Sodium 2mg Total Carbohydrate 0.2g Dietary Fiber 0g Total Sugars 0.1g Protein 0g

Creamsicles

Prep Time: 10 minutes

Cooking Time: 0 minutes

Freezing Time: 3 hours

Servings: 9

Ingredients:
- 1 can full-fat coconut milk
- ½ cup of water
- ¼ cup lemon juice
- 1 ½ teaspoons orange extract
- ½ teaspoon vanilla stevia
- 1 tablespoon sunflower lecithin powder

Directions:

1. Blend coconut milk, water, lemon juice, orange extract, stevia, and lecithin powder in a blender.
2. Divide the mixture into the popsicle molds.
3. Insert the popsicle sticks and freeze these popsicles for 3 hours.
4. Remove the popsicles from their molds.
5. Serve immediately.

Nutritional Values: Calories 58 Total Fat 5.6g Saturated Fat 5g Cholesterol 0mg Sodium 5mg

Total Carbohydrate 1.7g Dietary Fiber 0g Total Sugars 0.2g Protein 0.5g

Fudgesicles

Prep Time: 10 minutes

Cooking Time: 0 minutes

Freezing Time: 3 hours

Servings: 4

Ingredients:
- 1 (13.5 oz.) can full-fat coconut milk,
- 2 oz. dark chocolate, melted
- ¼ teaspoon vanilla powder
- ¼ teaspoon vanilla stevia

Directions:
1. Blend coconut milk, chocolate, vanilla powder, and stevia in a blender.
2. Divide the mixture into the popsicle molds.
3. Insert the popsicle sticks and freeze these popsicles for 3 hours.
4. Remove the popsicles from their molds.
5. Serve immediately.

Nutritional Values: Calories 70 Total Fat 6.5g Saturated Fat 5.4g Cholesterol 0mg Sodium 6mg

Total Carbohydrate 2.5g Dietary Fiber 1.3g Total Sugars 0.6g Protein 0.6g

Red White and Blue Popsicles

Prep Time: 10 minutes

Cooking Time: 0 minutes

Freezing Time: 6 hours

Servings: 4

Ingredients:

Red
- 1 cup of frozen strawberries

- ½ cup of water
- 1 teaspoon erythritol

White
- ½ cup full fat coconut milk
- 1 teaspoon choc zero maple syrup

Blueberry
- 1 cup frozen blueberries
- ½ cup of water
- 1 teaspoon choc zero maple syrup

Directions:
1. Blend strawberries with water and erythritol in a blender jug.
2. Divide the strawberry mixture into the popsicle molds.
3. Set these molds in the freezer for 1 hour.
4. Blend the coconut milk with maple syrup in the blender jug
5. Divide the white mixture in the popsicle molds.
6. Set these molds in the freezer for 1 hour.
7. Blend blueberries with water and maple syrup in a blender jug
8. Divide the blueberry mixture into the popsicle molds.
9. Insert the popsicle sticks and freeze these popsicles for 4 hours.
10. Remove the popsicles from their molds.
11. Serve immediately.

Nutritional Values: Calories 47 Total Fat 1.5g Saturated Fat 1.4g Cholesterol 0mg Sodium 2mg

Total Carbohydrate 9.9g Dietary Fiber 1.6g Total Sugars 7.1g Protein 0.4g

Lime Creamsicles

Prep Time: 10 minutes

Cooking Time: 0 minutes

Freezing Time: 4 hours

Servings: 6

Ingredients:
- 1 can full-fat coconut milk
- ½ cup mashed avocado
- ½ cup lime juice, freshly squeezed
- ¼ teaspoon vanilla stevia
- ⅛ teaspoon vanilla powder

Directions:
1. Blend coconut milk, avocado mash, lime juice, vanilla powder, and stevia in a blender.
2. Divide the mixture into the popsicle molds.
3. Insert the popsicle sticks and freeze these popsicles for 4 hours.

4. Remove the popsicles from their molds.
5. Serve immediately.

Nutritional Values: Calories 58   Total Fat 5.6g Saturated Fat 2.6g Cholesterol 0mg Sodium 3mg

Total Carbohydrate 2.1g Dietary Fiber 1.3g Total Sugars 0.2g Protein 0.6g

Blueberry Lime Popsicles

Prep Time: 10 minutes

Cooking Time: 10 minutes

Freezing Time: 4 hours

Servings: 8

Ingredients:
- 1 can coconut milk
- 1/2 cup blueberries
- 1/2-oz. lime juice
- 2 tablespoons mint leaves

Directions:
1. Mix blueberries and lime juice in a saucepan and cook for 5 minutes on medium-low heat.
2. Mix coconut milk with mint leaves in a saucepan and cook for 5 minutes then strain this milk.
3. Allow the mint milk to cool then divide it in the popsicle molds.
4. Place these molds in the freezer for 40 minutes until it is set.
5. Divide the berries mixture in the popsicle molds.
6. Insert the popsicle sticks and freeze these popsicles for 3 hours.
7. Remove the popsicles from their molds.
8. Serve immediately.

Nutritional Values: Calories 57   Total Fat 4.2g Saturated Fat 2.6g Cholesterol 15mg Sodium 4mg

Total Carbohydrate 4.6g Dietary Fiber 0g Total Sugars 4.2g Protein 0.2g

Peppermint Mocha Ice Cream

Prep Time: 10 minutes

Cooking Time: 10 minutes

Freezing Time: 6 hours

Servings: 6

Ingredients:
- 2 cups heavy whipping cream
- 2 oz. sugar-free dark chocolate, chopped
- 6 large egg yolks
- 2/3 cup powdered erythritol

- 2 tablespoons instant coffee powder
- 2 teaspoon vanilla extract
- ½ teaspoon salt
- 1 pinch food-grade peppermint extract
- 6 drops liquid stevia or to taste

Directions:
1. Beat and heat cream in a suitable pan on low heat.
2. Stir in chocolate and continue mixing until the chocolate is melted.
3. Add egg yolk and mix well until the whole mixture is heated through.
4. Stir in instant coffee powder, and sweetener then mix well.
5. Continue cooking this mixture for 10 minutes until it thickens.
6. Allow the ice-cream mixture to cool at room temperature.
7. Add salt, peppermint, stevia, and vanilla extract then mix well.
8. Transfer this ice-cream mixture to the ice-cream mixer.
9. Churn and freeze the ice-cream according to the machine's instructions.
10. Serve and enjoy.

Nutritional Values: Calories 196 Total Fat 19.3g Saturated Fat 10.8g Cholesterol 265mg Sodium 217mg Total Carbohydrate 1.9g Dietary Fiber 0g Total Sugars 0.3g Protein 3.5g

Vanilla Ice Cream

Prep Time: 10 minutes

Cooking Time: 10 minutes

Freezing Time: 6 hours

Servings: 8

Ingredients:
- 6 large eggs yolks
- 1 cup of coconut milk
- 1¼ cups unsweetened almond milk
- 1/3 cup xylitol
- 1/3 cup avocado oil
- 2 teaspoon vanilla extract
- 1/8 teaspoon salt

Directions:
1. Add almond milk and coconut milk to a cooking pot and set it over low heat.
2. Once the mixture is heated, stir in yolks, stir and cook until the mixture thickens.
3. Stir in sweeteners and mix well. Cook for another 10 minutes.
4. Allow the mixture to cool at room temperature.
5. Add salt, vanilla, and oil then blend the mixture with a blender.
6. Transfer this mixture to the ice-cream mixer.
7. Churn and freeze the ice-cream according to the machine's instructions.
8. Serve and enjoy.

Nutritional Values: Calories 125 Total Fat 11.4g Saturated Fat 7.3g Cholesterol 70mg Sodium 128mg Total Carbohydrate 3.1g Dietary Fiber 1.4g Total Sugars 1.3g Protein 3.5g

Mixed Nuts Ice-Cream

Prep Time: 10 minutes

Cooking Time: 0 minutes

Freezing Time: 5 hours

Servings: 8

Ingredients:
- 14 oz. half-and-half cream
- 12 oz. almond milk
- 14 oz. heavy whipping cream
- 16 oz. Cool Whip Topping
- 1 pinch saffron
- 1 teaspoon erythritol
- 1⁄2 cup mixed nuts, chopped

Directions:
1. Add erythritol and saffron to a mortar and blend with a mortar.
2. Beat half and half cream with milk, cream, and cool whip in a blender.
3. Stir in the saffron mixture and mix well.
4. Transfer this mixture to the ice-cream mixer.
5. Churn and freeze the ice-cream according to the machine's instructions.
6. Add nuts to the ice-cream and mix them evenly.
7. Freeze the nuts ice-cream again for 1 hour.
8. Serve and enjoy.

Nutritional Values: Calories 369 Total Fat 37.5g Saturated Fat 25.1g Cholesterol 88mg Sodium 67mg Total Carbohydrate 8.4g Dietary Fiber 1.3g Total Sugars 2.4g Protein 4.3g

Mason Jar Ice Cream

Prep Time: 10 minutes

Cooking Time: 0 minutes

Freezing Time: 3 hours

Servings: 2

Ingredients:
- ½ cup heavy whipping cream
- 1 egg yolk
- 1 tablespoon erythritol

- ½ teaspoon vanilla extract

Directions:
1. Add all the vanilla ice-cream ingredients to a mason jar.
2. Cover and seal the lid, then shake it for 5 minutes, vigorously.
3. Set this jar in the freezer for 3 hours.
4. Serve.

Nutritional Values: Calories 133   Total Fat 13.4g Saturated Fat 7.7g Cholesterol 146mg Sodium 16mg Total Carbohydrate 8.8g Dietary Fiber 0g Total Sugars 7.7g Protein 2g

Cookie Dough Ice Cream

Prep Time: 10 minutes

Cooking Time: 10 minutes

Freezing Time: 5 hours

Servings: 8

Ingredients:
- 1½ cups heavy whipping cream
- 1 cup unsweetened almond milk
- 5 large eggs yolks
- ½ cup xylitol
- 2 teaspoon vanilla extract
- ½ teaspoon salt

Cookie dough
- 2½ oz. almond flour
- 2 tablespoons xylitol
- 2 tablespoons butter, softened
- ½ teaspoon vanilla extract
- 1 tablespoon sugar-free baking chocolate, chopped

Directions:
1. Add cream and almond milk to a cooking pot and set it over low heat.
2. Once the mixture is heated, stir in yolks, stir and cook until the mixture thickens.
3. Stir in sweeteners and mix well. Cook for another 10 minutes.
4. Allow the mixture to cool at room temperature.
5. Add salt, and vanilla then blend the mixture with a blender.
6. Transfer this mixture to the ice-cream mixer
7. Churn and freeze the ice-cream according to the machine's instructions.
8. Mix all the ingredients for cookie dough in a suitable bowl.
9. Add the dough to the ice cream and mix well until evenly incorporated.
10. Freeze the ice-cream again for 1 hour.
11. Serve and enjoy.

Nutritional Values: Calories 323   Total Fat 33.9g Saturated Fat 20.9g 10 Cholesterol 121mg Sodium 83mg Total Carbohydrate 2.8g Dietary Fiber 0.2g Total Sugars 0.3g Protein 2.8g

Avocado Ice Cream

Prep Time: 10 minutes

Cooking Time: 0 minutes

Freezing Time: 4 hours

Servings: 6

Ingredients:
- 2 small ripe avocados
- 1 (8.5 oz) can full-fat coconut milk, unsweetened
- 2 tablespoons MCT oil
- Juice from 1/2 lemon
- 1/4 cup fresh basil leaves
- 1/4 cup fresh mint leaves
- 1 pinch of salt

Directions:
1. Blend avocado flesh, coconut milk, MCT oil, lemon juice, basil leaves, mint leaves, and salt in a blender jug until smooth.
2. Transfer this mixture to the ice-cream mixer.
3. Churn and freeze the ice-cream according to the machine's instructions.
4. Serve and enjoy.

Nutritional Values: Calories 119   Total Fat 11.1g Saturated Fat 3.4g Cholesterol 0mg Sodium 31mg Total Carbohydrate 5.3g Dietary Fiber 4g Total Sugars 0.3g Protein 1.1g

Neapolitan Popsicles

Prep Time: 10 minutes

Cooking Time: 0 minutes

Freezing Time: 4 hours

Servings: 6

Ingredients:
- 1 cup sour cream
- 1 cup heavy whipping cream
- 1/2 cup erythritol
- 1/2 teaspoon vanilla extract
- 1 cup chopped fresh strawberries, pureed
- 2 tablespoons cocoa powder

Directions:

1. Blend sweetener, ¾ cup whipping cream, sour cream, and vanilla extract.
2. Divide this mixture into three different bowls or containers.
3. Add the smooth strawberry puree to one bowl and mix well.
4. Add cocoa powder to another bowl and mix well.
5. Divide the cocoa cream mixture into the popsicle molds.
6. Then divide the white cream mixture in the molds.
7. Finally, top them with the pink strawberry cream mixture.
8. Insert the popsicle sticks and freeze these popsicles for 4 hours.
9. Remove the popsicles from their molds.
10. Serve immediately.

Nutritional Values: Calories 164 Total Fat 15.7g Saturated Fat 9.8g Cholesterol 44mg Sodium 29mg Total Carbohydrate 5.1g Dietary Fiber 1g Total Sugars 1.3g Protein 2.1g

Chocolate Peanut Butter Popsicles

Prep Time: 10 minutes

Cooking Time: 0 minutes

Freezing Time: 4 hours

Servings: 12

Ingredients:
- 8 oz cream cheese softened
- 1 cup creamy peanut butter
- 1/2 cup erythritol
- 1/2 teaspoon vanilla extract
- 3/4 cup heavy cream

Coating:
- 4 oz. sugar-free dark chocolate, chopped
- 1/2-oz. cocoa butter chopped

Directions:

1. Blend cream cheese, peanut butter, erythritol, vanilla extract, and cream in a blender.
2. Divide the mixture into the popsicle molds.
3. Insert the popsicle sticks and freeze these popsicles for 3 hours.
4. Meanwhile, melt chocolate and cocoa butter in a suitable bowl by heating in the microwave for 1 minute.
5. Layer a baking tray with a parchment sheet.
6. Remove the popsicles from their molds.
7. Dip each popsicle in the chocolate mixture and place it in the baking tray.
8. Freeze them again for 1 hour.
9. Serve immediately.

Nutritional Values: Calories 272 Total Fat 24.5g Saturated Fat 10.8g Cholesterol 31mg Sodium 163mg Total Carbohydrate 12.3g Dietary Fiber 2.6g Total Sugars 2.1g Protein 7.6g

Mocha Popsicle

Prep Time: 10 minutes

Cooking Time: 10 minutes

Freezing Time: 3 hours

Servings: 8

Ingredients:
- 3 cups full fat coconut milk
- 2 teaspoon grass-fed gelatin
- 1/2 cup Erythritol
- 1 teaspoon instant espresso powder
- 3 egg yolks
- 1/2 teaspoon vanilla extract
- 2 oz. sugar-free chocolate, chopped

Directions:
1. Mix coconut milk with gelatine in a saucepan and cook this mixture to a simmer.
2. Stir in instant coffee, sweetener, mix and cook until the temperature reaches 175 degrees F.
3. Beat the three egg yolks in a suitable bowl and stir in 1 cup hot coconut milk.
4. Mix well and return the mixture to the saucepan.
5. Cook for 5 minutes with occasional stirring then immediately transfer to an ice bath.
6. Allow the mixture to cool for 15 minutes.
7. Divide this mixture into the popsicle molds.
8. Insert the popsicle sticks and freeze these popsicles for 3 hours.
9. Meanwhile, melt chocolate in a suitable bowl by heating in the microwave for 30 seconds.
10. Remove the popsicles from their molds.
11. Drizzle chocolate over the popsicles.
12. Allow the chocolate set.
13. Serve immediately.

Nutritional Values: Calories 239 Total Fat 23.7g Saturated Fat 19.8g Cholesterol 2mg Sodium 11mg Total Carbohydrate 10.7g Dietary Fiber 1.1g Total Sugars 0g Protein 2.5g

Chocolate Avocado Pops

Prep Time: 10 minutes

Cooking Time: 0 minutes

Freezing Time: 3 hours

Servings: 8

Ingredients:
- 2 ripe avocados
- 6 tablespoon almond milk
- 1/4 cup erythritol
- 2 tablespoons cocoa powder
- 1/2 teaspoon vanilla extract
- 1/4 teaspoon stevia extract
- Pinch salt
- 2 oz. unsweetened chocolate, melted
- 2 tablespoons coconut oil, melted

Directions:
1. Blend and puree the avocado in the food processor for 3 minutes.
2. Add sweetener, cocoa powder, vanilla, stevia, salt, and almond milk.
3. Blend until smooth, then add the melted chocolate and coconut oil.
4. Mix well and divide this avocado mixture in the popsicle molds.
5. Insert the popsicle sticks and freeze these popsicles for 3 hours.
6. Remove the popsicles from their molds.
7. Serve immediately.

Nutritional Values: Calories 196   Total Fat 19.8g Saturated Fat 9.8g Cholesterol 0mg Sodium 26mg Total Carbohydrate 7.8g Dietary Fiber 5.2g Total Sugars 0.7g Protein 2.4g

Pina Colada Popsicles

Prep Time: 10 minutes

Cooking Time: 0 minutes

Freezing Time: 3 hours

Servings: 10

Ingredients:
- 11 oz. full fat coconut milk
- 1 ½ cup full-fat Greek yogurt
- 1/4 cup erythritol
- 1/2 teaspoon pineapple extract
- 1/4 teaspoon coconut extract
- 1/2 cup white rum

Directions:
1. In a blender, thoroughly blend the coconut milk, yogurt, erythritol, extracts, and rum until smooth.
2. Divide the mixture into the popsicle molds.
3. Insert the popsicle sticks and freeze these popsicles for 3 hours.
4. Remove the popsicles from their molds.

5. Serve immediately.

Nutritional Values: Calories 203   Total Fat 17.9g Saturated Fat 15.7g Cholesterol 1mg Sodium 16mg Total Carbohydrate 9.1g Dietary Fiber 0g Total Sugars 2.3g Protein 3g

Walnut Ice Cream

Prep Time: 10 minutes

Cooking Time: 10 minutes

Freezing Time: 6 hours

Servings: 8

Ingredients:
- ½ cups heavy whipping cream
- 5 large egg yolks
- 1 ½ cups almond milk
- 2 tablespoons erythritol
- ¾ cup choc zero maple syrup
- ⅛ teaspoon coarse salt
- ¼ teaspoon vanilla extract

Wet Walnuts:
- 1 ½ cups walnut halves
- ½ cup choc zero maple syrup
- 1 pinch salt

Directions:
1. Mix walnut halves with maple syrup and keep them aside for garnishing.
2. Add cream and almond milk to a saucepan and heat over medium heat.
3. Beat egg yolks with erythritol in a suitable bowl until pale and creamy.
4. Add half of the cream mixture to the eggs and mix well.
5. Return the mixture to the pan and cook until it thickens.
6. Transfer this mixture to the ice-cream mixer.
7. Allow the ice-cream mixture to cool then add remaining ingredients.
8. Churn and freeze the ice-cream according to the machine's instructions.
9. Garnish the ice-cream with maple walnuts.
10. Serve and enjoy.

Nutritional Values: Calories 150   Total Fat 13.6g Saturated Fat 2.4g Cholesterol 136mg Sodium 44mg Total Carbohydrate 6.7g Dietary Fiber 1.1g Total Sugars 4.7g Protein 5.6 g

Avocado Sorbet

Prep Time: 10 minutes

Cooking Time: 0 minutes

Freezing Time: 4 hours

Servings: 4

Ingredients:
- 3/4 cup avocado, diced
- 1/2 cup choc zero maple syrup
- 1/2 cup light coconut milk
- 1/4 cup fresh lime juice
- 2 teaspoons grated lime zest

Directions:
1. Blend and puree avocado flesh with syrup, coconut milk, lime juice, and zest in a blender.
2. Allow the ice-cream mixture to cool then add remaining ingredients.
3. Churn and freeze the ice-cream according to the machine's instructions.
4. Serve and enjoy.

Nutritional Values: Calories 126   Total Fat 12.5g Saturated Fat 7.5g Cholesterol 0mg Sodium 6mg

Total Carbohydrate 4.4g Dietary Fiber 2.6g Total Sugars 1.2g Protein 1.2g

Lemon Sorbet

Prep Time: 10 minutes

Cooking Time: 0 minutes

Freezing Time: 2 hours

Servings: 4

Ingredients:
- 1 ¼ cup water
- 3/4 cup granulated erythritol
- 1 strip of lemon peel
- Juice of 8 lemons
- Zest of 1 lemon

Directions:
1. Mix water with sweetener, lemon juice, and lemon peel in a blender.
2. Divide the mixture into the ice cubes molds.
3. Freeze the lemon ice for 2 hours in the freezer.
4. Now add the lemon ice-cubes to a blender and crush them at high speed.
5. Divide the crushed ice sorbet in the serving bowl.
6. Freeze until ready to serve.
7. Garnish with lemon zest.
8. Enjoy.

Nutritional Values: Calories 34   Total Fat 0.4g Saturated Fat 0.1g Cholesterol 0mg Sodium 5mg

Total Carbohydrate 10.8g Dietary Fiber 3.3g Total Sugars 2.9g Protein 1.3g

Berry Sorbet

Prep Time: 10 minutes

Cooking Time: 0 minutes

Freezing Time: 2 hours

Servings: 4

Ingredients:
- 1/2 cup 1 tablespoon granulated Erythritol
- 1/2 cup filtered water
- 3 tablespoons lime juice
- 2 cups fresh strawberries
- 2 cups fresh raspberries
- 1 tablespoon MCT oil

Directions:
1. Blend and puree raspberries with strawberries in a blender.
2. Pass the puree through a muslin cloth and discard the solids.
3. Mix water with sweetener and lime juice in a blender.
4. Stir in berries juice and MCT Oil.
5. Divide the mixture into the ice cubes molds.
6. Freeze the berry ice for 2 hours in the freezer.
7. Now add the berry ice-cubes to a blender and crush them at high speed.
8. Divide the crushed ice sorbet in the serving bowl.
9. Freeze until ready to serve.
10. Garnish as desired.
11. Enjoy.

Nutritional Values: Calories 53   Total Fat 0.5g Saturated Fat 0g Cholesterol 0mg Sodium 1mg

Total Carbohydrate 14.3g Dietary Fiber 5.7g Total Sugars 5.6g Protein 1.1g

Lemon Milk Popsicles

Prep Time: 10 minutes

Cooking Time: 0 minutes

Freezing Time: 3 hours

Servings:6

Ingredients:
- 1 cup of coconut milk
- 1 cup heavy cream
- 1 cup almond milk
- 1/2 cup erythritol

- 1/4 teaspoon stevia glycerite
- 2 tablespoons lemon juice
- Zest from 1 lemon
- 1 small pinch of salt

Directions:
1. Blend coconut milk, cream, and all other ingredients in a blender.
2. Divide this creamy mixture into the popsicle molds.
3. Insert the popsicle sticks and freeze these popsicles for 3 hours.
4. Remove the popsicles from their molds.
5. Serve immediately.

Nutritional Values: Calories 154 Total Fat 15.9g Saturated Fat 11.8g Cholesterol 27mg Sodium 37mg Total Carbohydrate 3.1g Dietary Fiber 0g Total Sugars 1.1g Protein 1.4g

Key Lime Popsicles

Prep Time: 10 minutes

Cooking Time: 0 minutes

Freezing Time: 3 hours

Servings: 6

Ingredients:
- 2 large ripe avocados
- zest from 1 lime
- juice from 2 limes
- 15 oz. coconut milk
- 1/2 cup powdered Erythritol
- 15-20 drops liquid Stevia

Directions:
1. Blend avocado flesh, lime zest, lime juice, coconut milk, erythritol, and stevia in a blender.
2. Divide this avocado mixture in the popsicle molds.
3. Insert the popsicle sticks and freeze these popsicles for 3 hours.
4. Remove the popsicles from their molds.
5. Serve immediately.

Nutritional Values: Calories 265 Total Fat 26.7g Saturated Fat 17g Cholesterol 0mg Sodium 14mg Total Carbohydrate 8.2g Dietary Fiber 4.9g Total Sugars 2.6g Protein 2.6g

Raspberry Chia Pops

Prep Time: 10 minutes

Cooking Time: 0 minutes

Freezing Time: 4 hours

Servings: 4

Ingredients:
- 1/2 cup lite coconut milk
- 1/2 cup unsweetened almond milk
- 3/4 cup raspberries
- 2 tablespoons chia seeds
- 1 tablespoon coconut, shredded
- 8 drops stevia

Directions:
1. Blend raspberries with almond milk, coconut milk, chia seeds, and stevia in a blender.
2. Divide this raspberry mixture into the popsicle molds.
3. Insert the popsicle sticks and freeze these popsicles for 4 hours.
4. Remove the popsicles from their molds.
5. Roll the popsicles in the coconut shreds.
6. Serve immediately.

Nutritional Values: Calories 56 Total Fat 3.6g Saturated Fat 1.9g Cholesterol 0mg Sodium 31mg

Total Carbohydrate 5.8g Dietary Fiber 3g Total Sugars 1.1g Protein 1.4g

Chocolate Cherry Ice Cream

Prep Time: 10 minutes

Cooking Time: 0 minutes

Freezing Time: 5 hours

Servings: 8

Ingredients:
- 1 cup heavy whipping cream
- 1 tablespoon erythritol
- ½ teaspoon cherry extract
- ¼ teaspoon almond extract
- 2 teaspoons juice from mixed berries
- 8 frozen dark unsweetened cherries

Chocolate Shell:
- ¾ cups of coconut oil
- 1 tablespoon erythritol
- 1-oz. unsweetened baking chocolate
- 3 tablespoons heavy whipping cream
- 1 tablespoon cocoa powder

Directions:

1. Blend cherries with cream, sweetener, extracts, and juice in a blender.
2. Divide this cherries mixture in the popsicle molds.
3. Insert the popsicle sticks and freeze these popsicles for 4 hours.
4. Meanwhile, melt chocolate in a suitable bowl by heating in the microwave for 1 minute.
5. Stir in cream, cocoa powder, erythritol, and coconut oil and mix well.
6. Remove the popsicles from their molds.
7. Roll and coat the popsicles with chocolate mixture.
8. Place these popsicles in a baking tray and freeze for 1 hour.
9. Serve immediately.

Nutritional Values: Calories 277 Total Fat 28.4g Saturated Fat 22.3g Cholesterol 21mg Sodium 7mg Total Carbohydrate 5.4g Dietary Fiber 3.8g Total Sugars 18.1g Protein 1.9g

Raspberry Ice Cream

Prep Time: 10 minutes

Cooking Time: 0 minutes

Freezing Time: 4 hours

Servings: 4

Ingredients:
- 2 cups raspberries
- 2 (400ml) cans of full-fat coconut milk
- 1/4 cup erythritol

Directions:
1. Blend raspberries, coconut milk and erythritol in a blender until smooth.
2. Transfer this mixture to the ice-cream mixer.
3. Churn and freeze the ice-cream according to the machine's instructions.
4. Serve and enjoy.

Nutritional Values: Calories 170 Total Fat 16.3g Saturated Fat 14.3g Cholesterol 0mg Sodium 10mg Total Carbohydrate 7g Dietary Fiber 2.7g Total Sugars 1.8g Protein 2g

Raspberry Mascarpone Popsicles

Prep Time: 10 minutes

Cooking Time: 1 minute

Freezing Time: 4 hours

Servings: 8

Ingredients:
- 1 cup mascarpone cheese
- 1 cup heavy whipping cream
- 2 cups frozen raspberries
- 1/4 cup powdered erythritol

- 10-15 drops liquid stevia
- 1 tablespoon sugar-free vanilla extract

Coating:
- 3 ½ oz. dark chocolate
- 1 oz almonds, chopped
- 1/4 cup freeze-dried raspberries, crumbled

Directions:
1. Blend all the mascarpone ingredients in a blender until smooth.
2. Divide this mascarpone mixture into the popsicle molds.
3. Insert the popsicle sticks and freeze these popsicles for 3 hours.
4. Meanwhile, spread almonds ground in one plate, and raspberries in another.
5. Melt the chocolate in a suitable bowl by heating in a microwave for 1 minute.
6. Remove the popsicles from their molds.
7. Dip the popsicles in the chocolate, almond, and raspberries.
8. Place the coated popsicles in a tray and allow the chocolate to set in the freezer.
9. Serve immediately.

Nutritional Values: Calories 212 Total Fat 17g Saturated Fat 9.7g Cholesterol 36mg Sodium 32mg

Total Carbohydrate 9.1g Dietary Fiber 3g Total Sugars 4.6g Protein 5.9g

Lemon Ice Cream

Prep Time: 10 minutes

Cooking Time: 0 minutes

Freezing Time: 3 hours

Servings: 6

Ingredients:
- 1 lemon, zest, and juice
- 3 eggs
- 1/3 cup erythritol
- 1¾ cups heavy whipping cream
- ¼ teaspoon yellow food coloring

Directions:
1. Separate egg yolks from their whites and beat the egg whites in a suitable bowl until fluffy.
2. Whisk eggs yolks with erythritol in a suitable bowl until it turns light in color.
3. Stir in yellow color, cream, and lemon juice, then beat again until fluffy.
4. Gently fold in egg whites and mix until uniformly incorporated.
5. Transfer this mixture to the ice-cream mixer
6. Churn and freeze the ice-cream according to the machine's instructions.
7. Or simply freeze the ice-cream mixture for 3 hours and stir it after every 30 minutes.
8. Serve immediately.

Nutritional Values: Calories 259 Total Fat 26.3g Saturated Fat 15.7g Cholesterol 171mg Sodium

56mg Total Carbohydrate 2.9g Dietary Fiber 0.3g Total Sugars 0.5g Protein 4.2g

Blueberry Ice Cream

Prep Time: 10 minutes

Cooking Time: 0 minutes

Freezing Time: 3 hours

Servings: 6

Ingredients:

- 1 cup heavy whipping cream
- 3 egg yolks
- 1 tablespoon erythritol
- ½ teaspoon vanilla extract
- ½ teaspoon ground cardamom
- ½ lemon, the zest
- 8 oz. mascarpone cheese
- 6 oz. frozen blueberries

Directions:
1. Beat cream in a suitable mixing bowl until it forms peaks.
2. Blend egg yolks with vanilla, cardamom, lemon zest, and erythritol in another bowl until fluffy.
3. Stir in mascarpone cheese and whipped cream.
4. Mix and add blueberries then stir well.
5. Transfer this mixture to the ice-cream mixer.
6. Churn and freeze the ice-cream according to the machine's instructions.
7. Or simply freeze the ice-cream mixture for 3 hours and stir it after every 30 minutes.
8. Serve immediately.

Nutritional Values: Calories 181   Total Fat 14.7g Saturated Fat 8.6g Cholesterol 152mg Sodium

44mg Total Carbohydrate 8.7g Dietary Fiber 0.9g Total Sugars 3.2g Protein 6.3g

Pink Cheesecake Popsicle

Prep Time: 10 minutes

Cooking Time: 0 minutes

Freezing Time: 3 hours

Servings: 6

Ingredients:
- 1 (8 oz.) block Cream Cheese
- 1/4 cup heavy whipping cream
- 10 large strawberries

Directions:

1. Blend cream cheese, cream, and strawberries in a blender.
2. Divide the mixture into the popsicle molds.
3. Insert the popsicle sticks and freeze these popsicles for 3 hours.
4. Remove the popsicles from their molds.
5. Serve immediately.

Nutritional Values: Calories 159 Total Fat 15.1g Saturated Fat 9.4g Cholesterol 48mg Sodium 114mg Total Carbohydrate 3.5g Dietary Fiber 0.6g Total Sugars 1.6g Protein 3.2g

Chocolate Popsicles

Prep Time: 10 minutes

Cooking Time: 5 minutes

Freezing Time: 4 hours

Servings: 6

Ingredients:

- 1 (13.5-oz.) can full-fat coconut milk
- 4 tablespoons erythritol
- 3 tablespoons cocoa powder
- 1/4 teaspoon kosher salt
- 1/8 teaspoon xanthan gum

Directions:

1. Mix coconut milk with cocoa, salt, and erythritol in a saucepan.
2. Cook the coconut milk mixture on a simmer for 5 minutes.
3. Stir in xanthan gum, mix well and cook until it is lump-free.
4. Divide the mixture into the popsicle molds.
5. Insert the popsicle sticks and freeze these popsicles for 3 hours.
6. Remove the popsicles from their molds.
7. Serve immediately.

Nutritional Values: Calories 117 Total Fat 12.4g Saturated Fat 10.9g Cholesterol 0mg
- Pinch salt
- 2 tablespoons butter, cut into two pieces
- 1 1/2 teaspoon vanilla extract
- 1/4 teaspoon xanthan gum

Strawberry Citrus Cheesecake Popsicles

Prep Time: 10 minutes

Cooking Time: 0 minutes

Freezing Time: 3 hours

Servings: 6

Ingredients:

- 8 oz cream cheese softened
- 1 cup cream
- 1/3 cup Erythritol
- 1/4 teaspoon stevia extract
- 1 tablespoon lemon juice
- 2 teaspoon lemon zest
- 2 cups fresh strawberries chopped,

Directions:

1. Blend cream cheese, cream, erythritol, 1 ½ cups strawberries, lemon juice, stevia and lemon zest in a blender.
2. Add remaining chopped berries and mix gently with a spatula.
3. Divide the mixture in the popsicle molds.
4. Insert the popsicle sticks and freeze these popsicles for 3 hours.
5. Remove the popsicles from their molds.
6. Serve immediately.

Nutritional Values: Calories 175 Total Fat 15.6g Saturated Fat 9.7g Cholesterol 49mg Sodium 126mg Total Carbohydrate 6.3g Dietary Fiber 1.1g Total Sugars 3.5g Protein 3.6g

Root Beer Popsicles

Prep Time: 10 minutes

Cooking Time: 0 minutes

Freezing Time: 3 hours

Servings: 10

Ingredients:

- 3/4 cup heavy whipping cream
- 1/4 cup erythritol
- 3/4 teaspoon vanilla extract
- 12 oz. sugar-free root beer
- 1/2 teaspoon root beer extract

Directions:

1. Blend cream with erythritol, vanilla extract, root beer, and root beer extract in a blender.
2. Divide the mixture into the popsicle molds.
3. Insert the popsicle sticks and freeze these popsicles for 3 hours.
4. Remove the popsicles from their molds.
5. Serve immediately.

Nutritional Values: Calories 61 Total Fat 3.3g Saturated Fat 2.1g Cholesterol 12mg Sodium 45mg Total Carbohydrate 8.7g Dietary Fiber 0g Total Sugars 7.2g Protein 0.2g

Raspberry Cream Popsicles

Prep Time: 10 minutes

Cooking Time: 0 minutes

Freezing Time: 3 hours

Servings: 6

Ingredients:
- 1 (14-oz) can full-fat coconut milk
- 6 tablespoon Erythritol
- 1/2 teaspoon coconut extract
- 10 oz. frozen raspberries
- 3/4 cup water

Directions:
1. Remove coconut cream from the top of the coconut milk and add to a bowl.
2. Stir in 2 tablespoons erythritol and coconut extract then mix well.
3. Blend berries with remaining erythritol and water in a blender.
4. Add the berries mixture to the coconut cream and mix only until it makes swirls.
5. Divide the raspberry mixture into the popsicle molds.
6. Insert the popsicle sticks and freeze these popsicles for 3 hours.
7. Remove the popsicles from their molds.
8. Serve immediately.

Nutritional Values: Calories 59   Total Fat 1.8g Saturated Fat 1.8g Cholesterol 0mg Sodium 3mg

Total Carbohydrate 9.5g Dietary Fiber 2.7g Total Sugars 4.7g Protein 1.5g

Coffee Ice Cream

Prep Time: 10 minutes

Cooking Time: 0 minutes

Freezing Time: 6 hours

Servings: 8

Ingredients:
- 2 ripe avocados, diced and frozen
- 13 oz. coconut cream, frozen into ice cubes
- 1 double shot of Bulletproof Coffee Espresso
- 2 tablespoons Lakanto Monk fruit sweeteners
- 1 teaspoon pure vanilla extract
- 1 tablespoon of Brain Octane Oil
- Coffee beans or chocolate chips, as a garnish

Directions:
1. Blend avocado flesh, coconut cream, coffee, lakanto, vanilla, and octane oil in a blender jug until smooth.
2. Transfer this mixture to the ice-cream mixer.
3. Churn and freeze the ice-cream according to the machine's instructions.
4. Garnish with coffee beans and chocolate chips.
5. Serve and enjoy.

Nutritional Values: Calories 225   Total Fat 21g Saturated Fat 11.8g Cholesterol 1mg Sodium 23mg

Total Carbohydrate 8.6g Dietary Fiber 4.4g Total Sugars 2.6g Protein 3.9g

Mint Chocolate Chip Ice Cream

Prep Time: 10 minutes

Cooking Time: 0 minutes

Freezing Time: 4 hours

Servings: 6

Ingredients:
- 1/2 cup heavy cream, whipped
- 1/2 medium avocado
- 1/2 teaspoon vanilla extract
- ½ teaspoon peppermint extract
- 1/2 teaspoon lemon juice, squeezed
- 1 pinch flakey sea salt
- 4 tablespoons powdered xylitol
- 1 (1.5 oz.) sugar-free chocolate chips

Directions:
1. Blend cream with avocado flesh, vanilla, peppermint, lemon juice, salt, and xylitol in a blender jug until smooth.
2. Fold the chocolate chips and mix until evenly incorporated.
3. Transfer the mixture to a sealable or lidded jar and freezer for 2 hours.
4. Garnish and serve in scoops.

Nutritional Values: Calories 107   Total Fat 8.7g Saturated Fat 4.5g Cholesterol 15mg Sodium

10mg Total Carbohydrate 5.7g Dietary Fiber 1.4g Total Sugars 3.8g Protein 0.9g

Strawberry Ice Cream

Prep Time: 10 minutes

Cooking Time: 0 minutes

Freezing Time: 6 hours

Servings: 6

Ingredients:

- 2 cans (13.5 oz) of coconut milk
- 16 oz frozen strawberries
- ½ tablespoon erythritol
- 1/2 cup fresh strawberries, chopped

Directions:

1. Blend coconut milk, erythritol, and frozen strawberries in a blender jug until smooth.
2. Transfer this mixture to the ice-cream mixer.
3. Churn and freeze the ice-cream according to the machine's instructions.
4. Fold in chopped fresh strawberries and mix evenly.
5. Freeze the strawberry ice-cream again for 1 hour.
6. Serve and enjoy.

Nutritional Values: Calories 182   Total Fat 17.1g Saturated Fat 15.1g Cholesterol 0mg Sodium 11mg Total Carbohydrate 8.4g Dietary Fiber 1.2g Total Sugars 4.2g Protein 2.1g

Bulletproof Ice Cream

Prep Time: 10 minutes

Cooking Time: 0 minutes

Freezing Time: 6 hours

Servings: 8

Ingredients:

- 4 whole eggs
- 4 egg yolks
- 2 teaspoon Vanilla Collagen Protein Powder
- 10 drops apple cider vinegar
- 7 tablespoon grass-fed butter
- 7 tablespoon coconut oil
- 3 tablespoons 2 teaspoons MCT oil
- 5 ½ tablespoon xylitol
- 1/2 cup of water
- 1/2 cup cocoa powder

Directions:

1. Blend eggs, yolks, and all other ingredients in a blender until smooth.
2. Transfer this mixture to the ice-cream mixer.
3. Churn and freeze the ice-cream according to the machine's instructions.
4. Serve and enjoy.

Nutritional Values: Calories 250   Total Fat 27.5g Saturated Fat 20.6g Cholesterol 213mg Sodium

116mg Total Carbohydrate 3.4g Dietary Fiber 1.6g Total Sugars 0.3g Protein 5.9g

White Christmas Ice- Cream

Prep Time: 10 minutes

Cooking Time: 0 minutes

Freezing Time: 12 hours 15 minutes

Servings: 8

Ingredients:
- 2 cups heavy cream
- 2 tablespoons granulated erythritol
- 1/2 cup desiccated coconut unsweetened, shredded
- 1 cup strawberries diced
- 2 tablespoons cacao nibs
- melted chocolate, to drizzle
- vanilla peppermint, orange or even brandy

Directions:
1. Beat cream with erythritol in a mixing bowl until it forms soft peaks.
2. Stir in cacao nibs, strawberries, and coconut and mix well with a spatula.
3. Transfer this creamy mixture to a pudding bowl and freeze it overnight.
4. To serve the ice-cream, flip this bowl on the serving plate.
5. Top it with melted chocolate and freeze again for 15 minutes.
6. Serve.

Nutritional Values: Calories 154   Total Fat 15.2g Saturated Fat 10.4g Cholesterol 41mg Sodium 14mg Total Carbohydrate 8g Dietary Fiber 1.6g Total Sugars 5.2g Protein 1.2g